Songs &

Songs entered in the U K Songwriting Contest 2020 & some of my poems

Barbara Burgess

Crowfoot Publishing

Barbara Burgess - Author

Barbara Burgess
Artist
Author
Songwriter
Psychic Medium
www.barbaraburgess.co.uk

Help The Author

Please support the author by doing the following:
 *Leave a review on Amazon
 *Give a copy of this book to loved ones, family and friends.
 *Randomly leave a copy of this book in a place where someone else might find it - a seat in a park - a table in a cafe. Random acts of kindness go a long way and are reciprocal.
 *Share the author's books and details with others:
 www.barbaraburgess.co.uk
 Amazon - https://tinyurl.com/jbxac2aa
 Thank you.

Copyright

Copyright © **Barbara Burgess 2021**
No part of this publication may be reproduced or transmitted in any form or future form or by any means or future means, including electronic, mechanical, photocopying, recording, or any other information storage or retrieval system without permission, in writing, of the author, apart from any permitted use under U K copyright law.

Please contact the author, Barbara Burgess via her website www.barbaraburgess.co.uk or use this email address: hello@barbaraburgess.co.uk

for written permission of use.

If you do not obtain written permission you are committing theft of the author's intellectual property.

All songs and poems in this book are copyright registered with SCO or GISC.

General Information

This book is all my own work.
There may be errors both typographical and grammatical.
The cover was created by V C BOOK COVER DESIGN

"Every song is like a painting."
    Dick Dale

Dedication

To my Family.
I love you with all my heart.
To all who love songs, singing and music and poetry.

And to all creatives.

Acknowledgements

I would like to thank the following:
    The Guild of Energists and all its members. It is like a family to me.

Dr. Silvia Hartmann, Sandra Hillawi, Wendy Fry.

The U K Songwriting Contest and all their Facebook page members for their encouragement.

The Songwriting Academy for their encouragement and courses.

Larissa, Selena and Richard for their encouragement and reviewing my songs and poetry.

Contents

Barbara Burgess - Author	3
Help The Author	4
Copyright	5
General Information	6
Untitled	7
Dedication	8
Acknowledgements	9
Untitled	13
Early Days	14
Little Whippet Pup	16
Moving On	18
They're Pulling The Houses Down In Luton Town	22
Train To Nowhere	24
Facebook Challenge	26
Another Challenge	28
Lockdown	30
Duette	34
Another Semi Finalist	38
Standing On My Own Two Feet	41
Something Different	44
Fourth Semi Finalist	47
Fast Paced	49
My Last Entry For 2020	52
Three Lockdowns	54
About The Author	60
Also By Barbara	62
Songwriting - Soundcloud	63
Barbara's Personal and Professional Qualifications	66
Contact	68

Untitled 69
1. Cover Image 70

"Funny how a beautiful song could tell such a sad story"
    Sarah Dessen

Early Days

I wrote poems from a very early age. However, the earliest poem I remember writing was one I called *Four Muddy Feet*.

The poem was about my Border Collie bitch Sue. I was about ten years old, 1956.

Tragically Sue died aged four. She had begun to have fits and there was one fit she did not come out of. I had come home from school in my dinner hour. I walked in the house and found mum crouched over Sue in the middle of a seizure. Sue had bitten her tongue and blood had splat all around the room, on the walls and the ceiling along with wee and poo that she had flapped her tail in. The whole scene was a disaster area. Mum said Sue had ben fitting for at least twenty minutes and she asked me to run to the phone box on the next street corner and phone for the vet. The vet arrived and put Sue to sleep to stop her suffering. I ran back to school in shock. My darling dog was dead.

I kept the poem *Four Muddy Feet* in a drawer in my

bedroom. Then, when I was at senior school and aged about eleven, 1957, there must have been an end of year competition. You could submit anything you liked. A piece of woodwork or metal work, a painting, some needlework. I submitted my poem.

By this my sister Christine had a Whippet called Sherry. I changed my poem title to *Little Whippet Pup* and put the name Pip in it as it seemed to fit well.

I recall the English teacher Mr Stanley Carter stopping me in the corridor and saying what a good poem it was. He then added that the last two lines did not rhyme perfectly. I knew they did not. Now as a seventy five year old adult in 2021, I realise they do not need to rhyme perfectly.

In those early days there were no computers. I might have borrowed a book that contained ideas for rhymes from our small local library or just used my head in order to get the rhymes. Nowadays one only has to do a Google search and you can come up with many rhyming suggestions.

Little Whippet Pup

Little Whippet Pup

Four muddy feet
And one wet nose

A hole in the garden
Where there should be a rose

A cry outside
A scratch at the door

A tired dog asleep
Curled up on the floor

Bones to chew
Slippers as well

What she'll find next

Songs & Poems 2020

We never can tell

She doesn't like baths
Loves a walk in the rain

She's a little Whippet pup
And Pip is her name

©Barbara Burgess - nee Ginn 1956

Moving On

On and off, throughout the following years I wrote numerous poems.

Some I submitted to newspapers and they were accepted.

I wrote about everyday life.

One day as I went to work on the bus I noticed that many houses were being pulled down and replaced by flats. Then I saw some shops and offices and factories being pulled down. I wrote the poem, *They're Pulling The Houses Down In Luton Town* and submitted it to the local newspaper, where it was accepted and printed.

The following day I recall the postman saying that he did not know I was a poet. I blushed as I thought of all those people reading my poetry. It is strange how some of us humans are afraid of success and being in the public eye but it happens to many of us. I am okay with it now.

In 2019 I discovered KDP or what was then known as Kindle Create. Due to the amazing rate in which technology was advancing ebooks were being made and sold and kindles had been invented.

You could have your own books placed on Amazon, for free, and you could collect the royalties. The word FREE appealed to me greatly.

I rummaged around in my bedroom and found most of the poems I had written over the years on scraps of paper and in notebooks. On 21st September 2019 I submitted my first poetry book to Amazon. *Afternoon Tea, To Make You Laugh, To Make You Cry, My Poetry.*

Then on November 2nd 2019 I submitted my second book of my poems. Coffee, Don't Mind If I do, My Poetry, Volume Two.

The first book was called Afternoon Tea as Richard and I had often met up with our daughters, Larissa and Selena, and celebrated things with an afternoon tea together.

The second book was called Coffee because my husband Richard was always drinking the stuff.

Then in 2020 the pandemic and lockdown began.

I was, at the time doing a course with Dr. Silvia Hartmann, president of The Guild of Energists. It was a course on Art and healing art.

The Modern Energy Art Course and Healing Art

It was a year long course done over the internet. This was very helpful as we were in lockdown. You could go for one walk a day and only go out for necessary shopping. Many people had time on their hands. I am so grateful for the internet and The Guild of Energists Courses.

One thing that I learned during the art course was that one did not have to be perfect, nor did your piece of artwork have to be perfect.

So often, in school and sometimes with parents and care

givers we are asked to do something again and again in order to make it better or to get it right.

One teacher asked me how I could get ten out of ten for my maths one week and then two out of ten the following week. Well a lot depends on what you are learning and how you take it in and also on your mood, whether you are happy or not. The happier a person is about a subject or in their everyday life then, the quicker they will learn.

I have trained dogs and the more excited and joyful a dog is then the easier it is for that dog to learn what you are teaching him.

It is all to do with energy. The higher your energy the happier you are and the easier it is to learn something or even to do something. I learned so much from The Guild of Energists and Silvia Hartmann and Sandra Hillawi over the years and it also helped me a great deal not only with my psychic work, my art but also with my songwriting.

Knowing that I and basically anything I did does not have to be perfect helped me to relax over the fact that the last two lines in my early poem, *Little Whippet Pup,* did not rhyme. I realised they didn't have to.

Later on I was to learn about rhyming, near rhyming and other kinds of poetic licence, as they call it.

One of the lessons in the art course was to create your own piece of music or song.

I did not create a specific piece for this lesson but meanwhile I had written the song *A Train To Nowhere.*

It is a strange fact but I knew this was a song and not a poem.

As I was growing up my mother used to read poems to us. She bought poetry books. One book of poems was by Rudyard

Kipling. Mum would recite the poems as she went about her daily chores.

Mum also had a great singing voice and she would sing while doing her chores.

We watched musicals together when the new fangled t v was invented. Before that we listened to music on the radio.

I also had ballet lessons and piano lessons. I believe that all these experiences helped me get a sense of rhythm. The beat of the music or the song.

As I was writing the song *A train To Nowhere* I had the beat of the train on the tracks in my head and the song just materialised.

Richard and I had gone to visit our younger daughter Selena and our Granddaughter Skye. We were at Ferry Meadows. We went on the little train there. The train sort of began nowhere and went nowhere and came back to nowhere. There was no station at either end of the track, so to speak and thus the song was born.

They're Pulling The Houses Down In Luton Town

They're pulling the houses down in Luton Town

They're pulling the houses down in Luton Town
They're pulling the houses down in Luton Town
Dear old Auntie Pat
Now lives in a top-floor flat
'cause they're pulling the houses down in
  Luton Town

They're pulling the old shops down in
  Luton Town
They're pulling the old shops down in
  Luton Town
Where I used to buy a bread roll
There's just a blooming' great hole
'cause They're pulling the old shops down in
  Luton Town

*They're pulling the factories down in
       Luton Town
They're pulling the factories down in
       Luton Town
They said, "no work today,"
And gave me two week's pay
'Cause They're pulling the factories down in
       Luton Town*

©*Barbara Burgess - nee Ginn 1963*

Train To Nowhere

On May 19th 2020 at 3.21pm I entered my song *Train To Nowhere* in the U K Songwriting Contest.
321 - is an angel number which means ask the angels to help you let go of your doubts and fears.

321 also means, ready, steady, go.

My first song entered in my first competition.

To my delight the song gained four stars commended and a certificate to prove it, in the lyrics section.

As I also had a tune to go with it I entered the song in the country section where it gained three stars.

My friend from the GOE (Guild of Energists and my tutor of many of my qualifications) told me that she had entered some songs in a competition and got into the finals. I searched for song competitions on the internet and found some in America and entered my songs there. They do not appear to give you results. You either win or don't win. Then I discovered The U K Songwriting Contest and have been entering my songs in that competition ever since.

Train to Nowhere

I'm on a train to nowhere,
Ticket in my hand.
I'm on a train to nowhere,
It's going to be grand.

I'm on a train to nowhere,
The window views are fine.
I'm on a train to no-where,
This day will be divine.

I'm on a train to nowhere,
Sunshine on my face.
I'm on a train to nowhere,
To avoid the human race.

I'm on a train to nowhere,
Destination – Mystery.
The sea, the hills, the countryside,
This train will set me free.

I'm on a train to somewhere,
Some where's where I'll be.
It's time out, time alone,
And time to spend with me.

Yes it's time out, time alone,
And time to spend with me.

©Barbara Burgess 2020

Facebook Challenge

Another friend of mine, Wendy Fry, who is also a member of The Guild of Energists and whom I met on a course, placed a post on Facebook one day. It began something like, "I woke up this morning."

I commented that it sounded like a song and Wendy challenged me to write the song.

And here it is. My second song to be entered in The U K Songwriting Contest.

This song gained four stars commended in the lyrics category and three stars in the folk category.

It seemed my songs did better in the lyrics section than with their melody. Still I continued to enter some songs with their melody as I felt they still stood a chance and I had the music in my head anyway.

I Woke Up One Morning

I woke up one morning

Songs & Poems 2020

*I opened my eyes
My hand held aloft
Blocked the sun from the skies*

*I sat in the darkness
I pondered o'er life
What is it all about?
Mostly trouble and strife.*

*For what you put in
Is what you receive
But don't let your worries
Your mind deceive.*

*So, I woke up this morning
And I opened my eyes
To the beauty that surrounds me
And God's gift surprise.*

*Yes, I woke up this morning
And I opened my eyes
To the beauty that surrounds me
And God's gift surprise.*

©Barbara Burgess 2020

Another Challenge

One category in the U K Songwriting Contest is to either make a new melody for an existing song or put new words to the old melody.

I took on this challenge and I changed the words of the song by Paul McCartney, Yesterday.

Here is my version of the new lyrics.

This entry gained five stars commended.

You can sing it yourself to the tune of Yesterday by Paul.

Oh My Love

Oh, my love,
You mean the very world to me.
I see you nightly in my dreams.
Oh love, life isn't what it seems.

You are gone,
And now I'm living on my own,

With nothing left me but my fate.
A painful heart about to break.

Oh, what can I do to bring you back to me?
I'd do anything for you are my destiny.

Oh, my love,
Won't you hear me when I cry,
For without you I know I will die.
Oh, please don't tell me it's goodbye.

Oh, what can I do to bring you back to me?
I'd do anything for you are my destiny.

Oh, my love,
Won't you hear me when I cry,
For without you I know I will die.
Oh, please don't tell me it's goodbye.

La, la, la, la, la, la, la.

©Barbara Burgess 2020

Lockdown

With the pandemic and lockdown life in general had changed dramatically. It was a whole new experience. The streets were empty. No cars on the road, no airplanes in the sky. The only shops allowed to be open were shops selling food. Everything else was shut by law.

The U K Songwriting Contest added anther category to their list and this was for a crisis song.

I wrote the following song and entered it in the lyrics only section where it gained five stars commended.

In the Love songs section, where I added the melody, it gained four stars commended.

In the crisis section along with the melody it received three stars.

And in the crisis, lyrics only section it won five stars commended.

Once again it appeared my songs did better in the lyrics only sections than when I added the melody.

Another thing I was learning about song writing was one

had to have *emotion* in the picture. One has to *move* someone, either to laugh or to cry. Which brings me back to my first poetry book - to make you laugh, to make you cry - My Poetry.

I recall a lady I did one of my first animal communication readings for. I did not know she was a writer and she sent me her book. It was a lovely book about her four dogs that had died suddenly. This author told me that a good book (and indeed a good song) will make someone laugh and cry.

Forever

Somehow, we'll be together,
come what may.
Somewhere we'll be together.
one fine day.
Someday we'll be together,
and forever we will stay,
in each other's arms,
I'm surrounded by your charms -forever -forever.

I know we'll be together,
come what may.
I know we'll be together,
one fine day.
I know we'll be together
and forever we will stay
beneath the shining stars,
this world will still be ours -forever -forever.

I know this is our destiny
There is no other wish for me -forever, and ever.

My love we'll be together,
come what may.
My love we'll be together,
one fine day.
My love we'll be together,
and forever we will stay,
by each other's side,
With you I will abide -forever -forever.

I know this is our destiny
There is no other wish for me -forever, and ever.

Somehow, we'll be together,
come what may.
Somewhere we'll be together.
one fine day.
Someday we'll be together,
and forever we will stay,
in each other's arms,
I'm surrounded by your charms -forever -forever.

I know this is our destiny
There is no other wish for me -forever, and ever.

I know this is our destiny
There is no other wish for me -forever, and ever.

Somehow, we'll be together,
come what may.
Somewhere we'll be together.
one fine day.

Songs & Poems 2020

*Someday we'll be together,
and forever we will stay,
in each other's arms,
I'm surrounded by your charms -forever -forever.*

©Barbara Burgess 2020

Duette

So then I got the notion to write a duet. I also fancied writing a song that had an Elizabethan air to it. I could imagine Henry VIII dancing with his lady to one of my songs.

I knew what I wanted to write but this song took a while to construct.

A Train To Nowhere and the songs that followed seemed to appear over night. Once inside my head they would not leave until I had written them down.

It was the idea of a duet that stayed in my head this time.

This particular song is about forbidden love.

It is my first song, in the lyrics only catagory, to gain five stars and be entered into the semi finals. I was elated.

I understand there were over 9,000 entries in 2020.

Lover's Duette gained a five stars and semi finalist award in the lyrics only section, giving me now three songs in the 2020 semi finals.

I was so excited and could not wait to hear if any of my songs has been accepted in the finals in 2020.

In the love songs category, Duette gained four stars commended. This version also included my melody for the song.

Duette gained three stars in the folk category.

It can be difficult to decide which category a song should go in. However, the organisers and judges say that if they think a song will stand a better chance in a different category then they place the song in that category.

In the open category Duette gained a four stars commended award.

Lovers' Duette

*My love you are the sweetest thing
that e'er did happen to me.
Oh, love you have the bluest eyes
that e'er mine own did see.*

*And love you have the softest skin
that mine own hands do touch.
I'll love you till the end of days,
to me you mean so much.*

*For you are mine and I am yours,
that's how it's meant to be.
For I am yours and you are mine,
together we will be.*

Barbara Burgess

True love as you lay in my arms,
your sweet breath on my brow.
I ask please will you marry me,
beneath the cherry bough?

My love I cannot marry you,
for I already wed.
And though we lay together here,
in our lovers' bed.

My heart is sold, my soul is gone,
but we together entwine.
And in your dreams, I'll be with you,
until the end of time.

For you are mine and I am yours,
that's how it's meant to be.
For I am yours and you are mine,
together we will be.

Oh, love I fear the seed is sown,
in my arms forever you'll be.
And I will take you for my own,
I love you desperately.

For you are mine and I am yours,
that's how it's meant to be.
For I am yours and you are mine,
through all eternity.

For you are mine and I am yours,

that's how it's meant to be.
For I am yours and you are mine,
through all eternity.

©Barbara Burgess 2020

Another Semi Finalist

So here I was in 2020 aged seventy four with having written only a handful of songs and now two of my songs had been awarded semi finals status.

The winning song for 2020 was actually written by a gentleman who was older than me. He was in his eighties and it was his first go at writing a song and his first go at entering a competition. Talk about beginner's luck.

So if you are a song writer or whatever it is you wish to put your hand to, then you are never too old. Remember that.

You are also never too old and it is never too late to try something new. If you don't try it then you will never know if you can do it or how good you are.

My mum climbed a mountain when she was about seventy five and the doctor told her off. She also gained her GCE in German when she was sixty five. My dad built houses until he was well into his nineties and he even put a new toilet in his flat when he was that age. He said it just took him a bit longer to do.

I had seen on The U K Songwriting Contest Facebook Page

that people sometimes put verse 1 and verse 2 and so on in their lyrics. So for some songs I began to do this.

Also The U K Songwriting Contest organisers allowed one to put notes along with their entry if they thought it might help their entry.

This song is a little bit about my emotions after losing our dog Zilzie, our Border Collie bitch. I write about her in my book *A Room Full of Love,* which is available on Amazon.

It can be difficult to decide which category a song should go in. However, the organisers and judges say that if they think a song will stand a better chance in a different category then they place the song in that category.

From Heaven I'll Watch Over You

Verse 1
Though you'll miss me when I'm gone
Though you'll cry from dusk to dawn
This I know is true
From Heaven I'll watch over you

Verse 2
Though your heart be filled with pain
Though you search for me in vain
This one thing I'll do
From Heaven I'll watch over you

Chorus
I know you'll feel lonely without me by your side
Things happen in life; we can't turn back
    the tide
I'll make up for all those nights when you cried

'cause being with you filled my heart with pride

Verse 3
There'll be times when you need my touch
To fading memories, you'll clutch
But this I promise you
From Heaven I'll watch over
From Heaven I'll watch over
From Heaven I'll watch over
You

This song could be written for an elderly person near the end of life OR a young person who is sick and near the end of life OR a dog or other pet that has died or is elderly.

©Barbara Burgess 2020

Standing On My Own Two Feet

And I was standing on my own two feet. I was gaining back my power.

My artistic talents seemed to have lain dormant for many years. Now due to writing a song for the GoE art course and possibly because I had time on my hands due to lockdown and wanted to do something to occupy my mind my artistic talents surfaced once more.

I began to do more art, more poetry and more songwriting.

This song became my third semi finalist in 2020, gaining five stars.

For some songs I continue to write verse 1 and verse 2 on my entry and I began to focus more on the lyrics only even though I always had a melody for my songs.

I feel the melody helped me to get the general rhythm of the song and was not necessarily a good enough melody to carry the song to semi finals or finals or even winning status.

Standing On my Own Two Feet

Verse 1
So many times, you did me wrong
I should have known you were bad all along
But baby now I'm feeling strong
I'm standing on my own two feet.

Verse 2
So many times, I loved you in vein
I should have known it would bring me pain
Now I'm in the sunshine, no longer in the rain
I'm standing on my own two feet.

Chorus
You filled my head with all your white lies
You filled my heart with your alibis
Don't you know now I'm wiser than wise?
'Cause I'm seeing you through brand new eyes

Verse 3
Now I'm gonna leave, it's the best thing yet
No, I won't be back, so don't you fret
And baby ain't gonna lose no sweat
I'm standing on my own two feet

Yes, I'm standing on my own two feet
I'm standing
Still standing
I'm standing on my own two feet

I'm Standing
Still Standing
Standing on my own two feet

Songs & Poems 2020

©*Barbara Burgess*2020

Something Different

With Lover's Duette I wanted to write something different and I continued wanting to do so.

I love sea shanties and country and western songs, jazz and just about any kind of song or piece of music. I was itching to write a different kind of song.

When you listen to some of the old songs that my mother used to sing, Such as Autumn Leaves - who would have thought of writing a song about Autumn or about leaves on a tree?

The following song, which won a five stars commended award in the lyrics only category, was one of my first efforts to write something a bit different. It took a while and I was pleased with the results and obviously the judges were as well.

In the open category along with the melody I had going around my head this song won four stars commended.

Let Me Mend Your Broken Heart

Let me mend your broken heart

Join the pieces one by one
Question is where do I start
Will I know when it is done

I'll take your trials and tribulations
Give you hope and expectations
Bring delight and joy a must
Bind together love and trust

So, let me mend your broken heart
Join the pieces one by one
Now that we have made a start
All your healing has begun

I'll take away your limitations
Bring you life's appreciations
Build affection and devotion
Take away all sad emotion

So, let me mend your broken heart
Join the pieces one by one
Now that we have made a start
All your healing has begun

I'll take your days and fill with bliss
Your old life you will not miss
Everything will start anew
All these things I promise you

Now let me mend your broken heart
Join the pieces one by one
Now that we have made a start

Barbara Burgess

Your new life has just begun

Oh, let me mend your broken heart
Join the pieces one by one
Now that we have made a start
Your new life has just begun

So, let me mend your broken heart
Please let me mend your broken heart

Oh, let me mend your broken heart
I can mend your broken heart

©Barbara Burgess 2020

Fourth Semi Finalist

Wow, what a proud songwriter I was when my next song became the fourth in 2020 to gain five stars and semi finals status in the lyrics only category.

I was now beginning to think of myself as a songwriter.

In the open category this song was awarded four stars commended status.

I was still trying to write something different, a different slant, a different rhythm than usual, just something that was just a bit different.

I was still not convinced I should begin entering lyrics only.

Love Is the Greatest Gift of All

I've had many lovers
But one thing I've discovered
That love is the greatest gift of all

When you're feeling down

Life's treating you like a clown
Your lover smiles and your doubts all fly away
A great day

He holds your hand
He understands
That love is the greatest gift of all

You're hurting inside
Pride keeps you from sharing
Your troubles
Your worries double

Then he comes along
With his magic wand

A kiss

And the world is a happier place
He wipes the tears from your face

Life has its moments of joys and of woes
Life's filled with highs and sometimes there's
    lows

And the hardest thing of all is when you fall
But love is the greatest gift of all

©Barbara Burgess 2020

Fast Paced

As I have mentioned I wanted to write something a bit different and I decided to try my hand at a faster paced song.

Here is Boom which gained four stars commended in the lyrics only section and four stars commended in the pop category.

Boom

Boom
You went and stole my heart

Boom
I loved you from the start

Boom
You set my soul on fire

Barbara Burgess

Boom
You are my heart's desire

I fell for you headlong
Now we have a love so strong
You're deep within my heart
And I know that we will never part

So
Boom
I'll love you till I die

Boom
Right up to the sky

Boom
Up to the moon and the stars

Boom
This love is always ours

I fell for you headlong
Now we have a love so strong
You're deep within my heart
And I know that we will never part

So
Boom
I'll love you till I die

Boom
Right up to the sky

Boom
Up to the moon and the stars

Boom
This love is always ours

So
Boom

©Barbara Burgess 2020

My Last Entry For 2020

My final entry for 2020 gained five stars commended in the lyrics only category.

I noticed a contestant on the group Facebook page with a lyrics entry and he had done well. I commented on his song and asked him if he ever put it in with the melody as well. He kindly replied that he only wrote the lyrics and not the melody in order to give his songs the best chance of getting into the finals and winning.

I then decided, even though I loved to add the melody, that I would enter in the lyrics only category in 2021.

Because Ive got You

I don't need no fancy Limousine
I don't need you to treat me like a queen
I don't need a day trip to a zoo
Because I've got you

I don't want a great big fancy house
I don't want you to treat me like a mouse
I don't want someone to cheer me when I'm blue
Because I've got you

I'm oh so glad I found you at last
Now I can say goodbye to my past
Living with you's gonna give me a blast
'cause loving you is all that I ask

I don't need no fond memories
I don't want no hurt remedies
I don't need nobody new
Because I've got you

©Barbara Burgess 2020

Three Lockdowns

On 31 December 2019, the World Health Organization was informed of a number of cases of pneumonia in Wuhan, Hubei Province, China. A new coronavirus, SARS coronavirus-2, covid-19, had been identified from patient samples.

Richard and I heard about this new virus through the news media but we never believed it would spread to the U K or the rest of the world as it has done.

Rumours were going around about how deadly it was but as we had not experienced anything like this before in our lives we found it unbelievable.

The Prime Minister, Boris Johnson advised everyone to keep at least two metres apart. We were also asked to wash our hands regularly for a minimum of twenty seconds. It was recommended that you sang *Happy Birthday* twice to yourself as this lasted for approximately twenty seconds. Face coverings were suggested and as I walked about when the law allowed me to I could see the occasional person wearing a face mask.

People in China and other foreign countries are often seen wearing face masks but for the general population of the U K it was something out of the ordinary and people felt uncomfortable as if they were thought of as wimps. The tough guys refused to wear masks even when it became compulsory.

And so it was on 23rd March 2020 the Prime Minister announced the first lockdown. We were told to 'stay at home'.

We were allowed to go for one walk a day and go out for any special provisions or see a doctor.

People began panic buying. Toilet paper was the first thing the shops ran out of.

My elder daughter Larissa lives in Queensland, Australia and she says that whenever there is an announcement of a hurricane the first thing people rush to buy is toilet paper. She now keeps her own stack in her cupboard as often the shops are empty.

Stores then began to restrict the number of items a person could buy at one time to three of the same item.

I decided to have our weekly shop delivered but delivery slots were few and far between. Even being able to register on a shopping site, such as Asda or Sainsbury was virtually impossible.

Our younger daughter Selena already had her shopping delivered and she managed to get Richard and me two shopping loads.

Richard then received a letter from the Prime Minister stating that as he was recovering from pancreatic cancer and had other health issues he was listed as 'highly vulnerable'. This meant that should he catch the virus then it could have disastrous results.

Being listed as highly vulnerable meant that we could have a priority shopping slot on the major supermarket websites.

This did take a while to come into action but meanwhile we had the two deliveries that Selena had kindly organises.

The Prime Minister had also set up weekly deliveries of essential foods such as bread, milk potatoes and other goodies for the elderly and vulnerable. We had two deliveries of these boxes and were very grateful to the government for thinking up this idea.

Everyone was now living in a totally unknown world and people were panicking and getting stressed out.

Our slots with the big supermarkets began to come through and we then had a regular food delivery each week. Sometimes it was difficult to get a food slot and so I had to juggle between different supermarkets but on the whole we did very well and got all the food we needed for ourselves and our Border Collie dog Mitch.

We cancelled the weekly food box from the government as this then went to another needy family.

One thing I will mention here is that when I was out with walking my dog for my one walk a day I saw a man on a regular basis looking in the bins around the town. As we were not supposed to go near people I left a note on one of the bins I regularly saw him rummaging through letting him know where he could find a food bank. I also noticed once or twice a carrier bag of food near the bin and someone was looking after him. The man did not look English.

So many people were finding it hard to make ends meet. People could not go to work. Shops and businesses had to close and people had to stay at home.

A man wrote to me and asked me what was going to happen to him and his children. I wrote back as best I could and sent him and his family healing and said a prayer for them.

As Richard came under the extremely vulnerable label he

was asked to stay at home and not even go for the one daily walk.

Just before the lockdown began our toilet broke. Richard had mended it before but now it refused to flush. The sink had had a small crack in it since the day we moved in. Richard decided to have a new bathroom suite delivered. We knew nothing then that lockdown would happen but when it did and Richard had to stay at home he began to put the new bathroom suite in and luckily that kept him and his mind occupied.

Richard also laid a new floor in the bathroom and the lobby and did some tidying up as he went along. The previous owners must have been DIY people and as Richard is a qualified tradesman he likes things to be correct.

During the three lockdowns that we had Richard did the bathroom and other odd jobs around the house, fixed the fences in the garden and enlarged what we call the Wendy house at the bottom of the garden and moved the shed to the other side of the garden. So he was able to keep himself busy.

Later on we were allowed to go for two walks and so Mitch was happy about that.

Slowly life got back to the new normal. It would never be the same again. People keeping away from people when they are used to mixing and chatting with other.

People were afraid as well. Often someone would cross the road or walk in the road to avoid me and Mitch.

It was rumoured that animals and especially dogs could spread the virus and a lady who often stroked Mitch stopped doing so. She apologised to Mitch and said she was sorry but she could not stroke him.

While all this lockdown business was going on I continued with my song writing and the courses I had enrolled on.

One day when I was Googling The U K Songwriting

Contest I accidentally clicked The Songwriting Academy. There on there first page was an advert for an online course on songwriting. It had been reduced from about two hundred pounds to five pounds. I could not believe my eyes and signed up to it immediately.

It was an excellent course, great fun and I learned much along the way.

During the course on Zoom, we went to different 'rooms' and joined about four other people and we were asked to write a song together each time. This we managed and I enjoyed taking part in this immensely.

Then I joined a group on Facebook who also got together to write songs but for me this did not work as well. I felt pressurised into producing lyrics on the spot and it did not suit me.

I find I need to sit quietly or go for a walk in the woods or the countryside in order to be creative.

Another thing that happened was after my dad passed away. I went and had my eyes tested and the optician said I had holes in both my retinas. I made several trips to the hospital and my left eye hole has got as big as it can be and the right eye has the hole just beginning.

The specialist told me that there have been occasions when a person's eyes have righted themselves and I plan to be one of those one in three thousand people. Indeed I met a man on the tram going back home who overheard Richard and me talking about my eyes and he said his eyes had healed themselves. There was hope for me yet.

Because of my eyesight, where it often looked as though I was seeing things through water, I decided to sell my car. I felt it was too dangerous to drive. This meant that I could not take Mitch out into the woods on a daily basis any more and not have my quiet and peaceful creative moments anymore. However we do go for long walks and I have managed to find some routes to some wooded areas.

During the pandemic and after the three lockdowns I also decided to buy myself a piano. I also bought a course by Stephen Ridley. It is an excellent course on how to play the piano. The course is set out in a methodical manor so that it is easy to learn and so that anyone can progress well and learn to play the piano.

I am, in a way, grateful for the time lockdown gave me. It changed my perspective on life as it probably has done for many people.

Many people now have different jobs. Many people work online rather than travelling to and from work in busy traffic and on busy public transport all the time. Many people also have found ways of working with others all around the world. Our world has definitely changed due to this pandemic and for some it has changed for the better.

My heart goes out to all those who have suffered during the pandemic and lost loved ones.

About The Author

From a very early age Barbara has enjoyed writing poetry and prose.
 Barbara Burgess began writing her first novel at about the age of ten. It was a story about how a dog rescued a little boy. Barbara did not have a clue about publishing and she sent her written copy off to some publishers. She had a very nice letter back saying that they rarely read unsolicited manuscripts

but had read hers. They said it had a good beginning and a good ending, but the middle needed some improvement.

At a very young age Barbara also had some poems printed in the local newspapers.

Barbara has enjoyed writing poetry, short stories and self help books for many years now. She currently has written about sixteen books.

Barbara continues to write short stories, songs, and poems and enjoys art and playing the piano.

Also By Barbara

Afternoon Tea. To Make You Laugh, To Make You /Cry, My Poetry

Coffee? Don't Mind If I Do. My Poetry, Volume Two

A Funny Thing Happened On My Way to the Church

You will find Barbara's books on Amazon.com and Amazon.co.uk

Songwriting - Soundcloud

I have been writing poetry since I was about ten years of age. I have had some poems published in local newspapers, also from a very early age.

I have self published, under my publishing name - Crowfoot Publishing - two books of my poetry - Afternoon Tea, To Make You Laugh, To Make You Cry, My Poetry and Coffee? Don't Mind If I do, My Poetry Volume Two.

Afternoon Tea was written because we, as a family, often had afternoon tea together.

Coffee? Was written because my husband Richard used to drink gallons of the stuff and our younger daughter, Selena also loves to drink coffee.

My mother had a lovely voice. She was always singing. We also watched films and tv shows that contained music and songs and we listened to songs on the radio. My dad bought a record player and we started to listen to records. Mum had Bolero which had a scratch halfway through the first side of the record and you had to move the needle and miss a bit of the music.

Then you had to turn the record over to listen to the rest of the piece. We also had 1812 Overture on a black vinyl record. I loved those pieces.

I began playing the piano and the organ at about age sixteen or maybe younger. I was told I was very good but when it came to exams I was petrified and so stopped going to lessons.

It wasn't until I took the Modern Energy Art and Art Therapy course with Silvia Hartmann in 2019 that I began to rekindle my love of music. As part of the course one had to write a song.

About that time I was with our granddaughter Skye and younger daughter Selena and husband Richard at a park. We went on the miniature railway. This made me think of a song - Train To Nowhere. It just came into my head, out of the blue.

My friend and GoE Trainer Sandra Hillawi wrote songs and poems and told me that one of her songs had got into the finals of a competition. I looked around for song and poetry competitions and found The John Lennon Song Contest. I entered my song but heard nothing back about whether or not I had won. The winners and runners-up won equipment like guitars and speakers and such like.

Then another friend of mine on social media, Wendy Fry, posted something about 'I woke up this morning.' I replied to the post that it sounded like a song and Wendy challenged me to write one. This I did. I wrote - I Woke Up One Morning.'

I then found The U K Songwriting Contest on Google and entered both these songs, my very first, and was totally amazed that I got Four Stars, Commended for the lyrics of Train To Nowhere and Three Stars for the version with the melody.

I received Four Stars, Commended for, 'I Woke ~Up One Morning' lyrics and Three Stars for the song with the melody. I was over the moon! It spurred me on and I continued to write more songs.

Oh My Love - gained Five Stars, Commended. This song was for a challenge where you write new words to the tune of Paul McCartney's 'Yesterday'.

Forever gained Five Stars, Commended in the lyrics section, Four Stars Commended in the Love songs Section. Three Stars and Five Stars Commended in other sections.

'Lover's Duette', 'From Heaven I'll Watch Over You', 'Standing On My Own Two Feet' and 'Love Is The Greatest Gift Of All' gained SEMI FINALS STATUS with Five Stars, Commended. A great achievement for my very first attempts at song writing. I am so thrilled. The Semi Finalist songs also won several other awards.

Three more songs, 'Because I've Got You', 'Boom', and Let Me Mend Your Broken Heart', also won several Star Awards and Commended.

A thrilling experience to say the least.

I continue to write songs and poems.

Here is a link to my Sound Cloud page:

soundcloud/barbara-avril-burgess

https://soundcloud.com/barbara-avril-burgess/sets/u-k-songwriting-contest

Barbara's Personal and Professional Qualifications

Barbara's personal and professional qualifications:
At school:
GCE in Maths, English and Geography.
Pitman's Elementary Typing and Shorthand.
On Leaving school:
The Complete Piano Masterclass - Ridley Academy (age 75)
Songwriting - The Songwriting Academy (age 74)
Reiki Master
Seichem Master
Hypnotherapy
Counselling
Certificate of Clairvoyance
Certificate of Tarot
Animal Healing
Angel Card Reader
Realm Reader
Mediumship

Medical Intuitive
Crystal Healing
Spiritual Healing
Intuitive Feng Shui
Louise Hay, Heal Your Life Teacher
Freeway CER (similar to EFT)
EFT - Emotional Freedom Technique
Tapas Acupressure Technique (TAT)
Guild of Energists (GoE) Money
GoE Star Matrix Master
GoE Supermind Master
GoE Modern Energy Art Master and Modern Energy Art Therapy
GoE Energy Symbols Master
EMO - Emotional Transformation now known as EmoFree

Contact

Barbara Burgess
www.barbaraburgessauthor.com

barbaraburgess7@gmail.com

"I don't force it. If you don't have an idea and you don't hear anything going over and over in your head, don't sit down and try to write a song. You know, go mow the lawn... My songs speak for themselves."
    –Neil Young

Chapter 1

Cover Image

The cover image was created on Picsart.

Printed by Amazon Italia Logistica S.r.l.
Torrazza Piemonte (TO), Italy